T0652630

HAPPY
WARRIOR

YOUR PRACTICAL GUIDE
TO A HAPPY LIFE

HAPPY
WARRIOR

Empower Your S.E.L.F. in 30 Days

JAMI BERTINI &
JOHN KALINOWSKI

Selfscription® Press
New York, New York

Copyright © 2019 by GrowVision LLC / John Kalinowski & Jami Bertini

All rights reserved. This book or any portion thereof may not be reproduced or used in any manner whatsoever without the express written permission of the publisher except for the use of brief quotations in a book review or scholarly journal.

DISCLAIMER: The authors of this book do not dispense medical advice or prescribe the use of any technique as a form of treatment for physical, emotional, or medical problems. The intent of the authors is only to offer information of a general nature to help you in your quest for emotional and spiritual well-being. In the event you use any of the information in this book, which is your constitutional right, the authors and the publisher assume no responsibility for your actions. Thank you.

ISBN: 978-1-7345276-0-5

Library of Congress Control Number: 2020900970

Note from the Authors

The foundations for **Happy Warrior**, and its parent company, Selfscription®, all started in a marketing class at NYU, where we met while both pursuing our coaching dreams. Through many ups and downs, starts and stops, we persevered. Of course, none of this would be possible without the power of love to conquer fear.

We dedicate this book to all of our family, friends, clients, and guides who continue to love and support us on this great adventure.

Onward and upward!

John & Jami

Welcome!

We're excited you're here.

We are NYU-certified coaches, authors, speakers, and mindset experts with nearly two decades of coaching experience between us. We joined forces in 2013 to write Selfscription® Mindset, a coaching journey and workbook, which we have been using with our private clients for several years. We have empowered individuals from all over the world to elevate their consciousness, and we are now bringing these powerful tools and practices to you.

In 2018, Selfscription® expanded to feature books, notebooks, workbooks, inspirational quotes, and individualized coaching, all designed to take your happiness journey to the next level.

Let's get started!

John & Jami

A percentage of all proceeds from Selfscription®
products will be donated to the Ali Forney Center,
a non-profit organization created to "protect LGBTQ youth
from the harms of homelessness and empower them
with the tools to live independently."

What does it mean to be a Happy Warrior?

Happiness is not just a feeling; it's a mindset and a way of life. It means making a choice to accept and be grateful for ourselves and the people around us. It means that we choose to be purposeful and thoughtful in all areas of our lives. And it means that we are choosing to see how life might actually be happening *for* us, instead of *to* us.

A Happy Warrior is a person who navigates life with intention, kindness, and courage. A Happy Warrior fights the good fight of choosing love over fear, over and over again. Choosing to operate from love is simple, but not easy. The further a Happy Warrior travels on their journey, the more elaborate the life lessons become. A Happy Warrior doesn't give up; they keep growing and evolving.

Happy Warriors travel through life gently; they don't force life to happen. Instead, they allow life to unfold. They listen to their heads and their hearts and make decisions based on logic, as well as what feels right inside of them. Happy Warriors experience the challenges of life just like everyone else, but they handle the challenges, feel their feelings, and they make happiness and love their true north.

Happiness is not something we can buy or sell, and it's not acquired through a particular accomplishment or event. Happiness is inside each one of us and can be ours at any moment when we decide to embrace it. There is plenty of Happiness for everyone; it never runs out. Happiness is a choice. And the choice is yours.

This is what it means to choose happiness. This is what it means to empower yourself and walk the path of a Happy Warrior.

Elevate Your S.E.L.F.

"Elevate Your Consciousness … and your
world will never be the same."
—Selfscription®

You are embarking on a happiness journey that will open your heart and mind in ways you never thought possible. Each day of this journey is intended to help you detach from your thoughts and make you more aware of your impact on the world. By doing so, you will not only create a deeper, more sustainable level of inner peace, but you will find that life becomes happier, more fluid, and more fulfilling overall.

Mindset Shift:

- Learn to see your SELF based on your internal vs. external accomplishments.
- Reflect on your choices as a means of clarifying the outcome you desire.
- Learn to make decisions based on love instead of fear.
- Start to feel the effects of living a balanced life.
- Feel less stress and anxiety.
- Live in the moment.
- Feel empowered.
- Free Your Mind.

Contents

Notes from Yourself:

Once you see, you cannot unsee.

Love,
Yourself

SO, IT BEGINS...

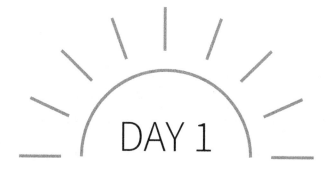

DAY 1

The Commitment

Welcome, Happy Warrior!

Notes from Yourself:

*You can do anything,
once you commit to it.*

Love,
Yourself

You are a Happy Warrior...

The first step in living life as a Happy Warrior is learning how to create happiness and inner peace just by knowing how to manage and detach from your thoughts and emotions. Feeling happy isn't about anything external. It's not about the perfect job, or the perfect relationship, or anything else you can acquire.

Living life as a Happy Warrior is rooted in developing a happiness mindset, which is based on these Top 5 Core Values: Mindfulness, Coaching, Freeing Your Mind, Elevating Your Consciousness, and Taking Your Life to the Next Level. A happiness mindset represents a new way of looking at your life. Each of The Top 5 Core Values allows you to prioritize the development of your higher, most evolved, happy self.

Walking the path of a Happy Warrior supports your choices and growth toward living the happiest life possible. You will become an observer and organizer of your inner world while learning to better manage and elevate your impact on the world around you.

"Happiness is a mindset."
—Selfscription®

Notes from Yourself...

On each day, you will see a note from your inner voice giving you a daily dose of love and inspiration. Each note is not only an introduction for the day's mindset shift but also food for thought to reflect on throughout the week.

"You have all your answers."
—Selfscription®

Top 5 Core Values of a Happy Warrior

1. Mindfulness: being aware of your thoughts, your feelings, and your impact on yourself and others.

2. Coaching: checking in, questioning yourself, your thoughts, your feelings, and your impact on the world around you.

3. Freeing Your Mind: freeing yourself from the regrets of the past and worries of the future.

4. Elevating Your Consciousness: operating from a higher intellectual and spiritual awareness.

5. Taking Your Life to the Next Level: achieving external rewards as a result of internal growth.

Happy Warrior: Take yourself through Getting Started, below, to give yourself a sense of what will be expected from you on your happiness journey. It all goes back to the setup. This means that how you start something sets the tone for the entire experience.

Getting Started...

"It works if you work it, regardless of how long it takes you to work through it."
—Selfscription®

You are embarking on a happiness journey to explore who you are and what you want. Some concepts take longer to master than others. Just stick with it—it works if you work it.

Plan a time and place to work on your daily mindset shift. Each session will take anywhere from five to twenty minutes. Take each session's tools and personal insights and incorporate them into your daily life.

Prior to each session, clear away any distractions, such as your phone, computer, etc. You deserve this time for *you*!

Journal your thoughts, feelings, insights, hopes, and dreams daily. Having a journaling practice helps you gain clarity, resolve issues, and incorporate a happiness mindset.

If you happen to fall off of the 30-day schedule, that's okay! Don't beat yourself up; just make a decision to come back to it. This is your journey and you are in charge of the pace. You will get all the benefits of each exercise as long as you show up and do it!

You are on a journey of self-discovery. At times, it can be enlightening, and other times it can be uncomfortable. No judgment! You Are Enough.

To help you get the most out of your journey, you can also pick up the accompanying Pocket Planner and Reflection Journal on Selfscription.com.

Let's do this!

Happy Warrior: Below are a few thoughts on why we love to record our reflections through journaling and doodling. You will also want to integrate these practices into your daily rituals.

Reflections

Journaling & Doodling

Strengthen Your Internal Journey: Journaling and Doodling invoke Mindfulness and help you to remain present while shifting your perspective. They provide clarity and help you to gain a greater sense of confidence and self-identity.

Think in Big-Pictures: When you are too focused on drama and details, you can overthink. Journaling and Doodling help you to get out of your thoughts, take a step back and focus on the bigger picture.

Reduce Your Stress: Journaling and Doodling calm anxiety and reduce the negative impact of stress on your mental and physical health.

Boost Your Mood: Journaling and Doodling can improve your mood and give you a greater sense of overall emotional well-being and happiness.

Keep Your Brain Sharp: Journaling and Doodling help boost memory, focus, and comprehension and improve cognitive processing.

Happy Warrior: Read, sign, and date "The Commitment" below, which creates accountability and reinforces your dedication to the thirty-day journey as a launching pad for the journey beyond.

The Commitment

You've said, "Yes!" to an exploration into who you are and what you want. This happiness journey will enable you to Free Your Mind and Take Your Life to the Next Level.

Everything you want to create in your life is dependent upon becoming the observer of your thoughts and feelings, harnessing your energy, and believing that you are enough.

Do you want to be happy?

- Do you want to be successful?
- Do you want to feel like you have made your mark?
- Do you want to have a loving, fulfilling relationship?
- Do you want to be surrounded by people who care about you?

The surest way to do all of those things starts with observing your thoughts, shifting your habits, and building your sense of self. As long as you stay disciplined, you will acquire tools and practices that will last you a lifetime. It all starts with your thoughts…

I, _____, will show up for my happiness journey.

Sign _____ Date _____

DAY 2

The Setup

Notes from Yourself:

It all goes back to the setup.
Without the proper setup,
you will run into snags.

Love,
Yourself

Happy Warrior: Here we go!

Starting Point

The Starting Point provides you with a snapshot of where you are now. Rate each question below, with 1 being the lowest and 10 being the highest, and describe what it means to you.

On a scale of 1–10, how happy are you right now?

_____

_____

_____

On a scale of 1–10, how willing are you to be 100 percent honest with yourself?

_____

_____

_____

On a scale of 1–10, how open are you to looking at your life from a new perspective?

_____

_____

_____

On a scale of 1–10, how willing are you to stretch your comfort zone?

_____

_____

_____

What percentage of your time is spent being open vs. being closed to yourself and to what life has to offer?

_____

_____

Happy Warrior: Set your Intention for what you want to walk away from this happiness journey with. Visualize how this will impact your life.

Intention

Achieved By: _____, _____, _____ (Date)

What is your Intention for this journey?

Intention is the energy that drives you toward your goals. How do you want to feel? Who do you want to be? Boil it down to a word or phrase that you find energizing and empowering. This is your Intention.

_____

_____

_____

Visualization:

How do you see your life shifting as a result of achieving this Intention?

_____

_____

_____

_____

_____

_____

_____

_____

_____

_____

_____

_____

Reflections

Journal:

Doodles:

DAY 3

What Is Coaching?

Notes from Yourself:

Coaching is a process designed to help you engage your mind, clarify your vision and Take Your Life to the Next Level.
You got this!

Love,
Yourself

Happy Warrior: As a Happy Warrior, it's important to be "coachable," meaning that you are able to move through your thoughts to make empowered choices that create the outcomes you desire. Coaching yourself also helps you recognize when you are getting in your own way or holding yourself back.

Coaching is an internal process of self-discovery, designed to help you engage your mind, clarify your vision, and Take Your Life to the Next Level. Coaching helps you to cultivate more awareness in your daily life, enabling you to better assess your thoughts, behavior, and your impact on the world around you. In other words, Coaching will help you strengthen your relationship with yourself and everything else. By asking yourself more powerful questions and listening to yourself more intently, you will start to trust yourself in a way that you've never trusted yourself before.

By Coaching yourself and keeping track of questions and Affirmations you find impactful, you can peel back the layers of stories and beliefs you've carried for years. Instead of living your life as a victim of old programming that no longer serves you, you become the creator of your own life. It is through this internal Coaching process that you will begin to affect greater change in the external areas of your life, such as work, romance, friendship, finances, and even your body. Not only will you be clearer, calmer, and happier, you will also start to see solutions in various places where you may have felt stuck. This is the foundation on which to build a clear life vision, chart a course to achieve all of your goals, and walk the path of a Happy Warrior.

Happy Warrior: Coach Yourself. Use the Self-Coaching questions below to coach yourself through a challenge you may be facing or a decision you need to make. You can use these questions in a pinch, with yourself or with others.

Self-Coaching Questions:

- What can I give to this situation versus what can I get from it?
- Am I repeating a pattern?
- How does knowing what I know now influence my decision?
- What beliefs do I hold that are limiting me?
- How can I clean up my side of a relationship?
- What am I willing to Let Go of?

Self-Coaching Affirmations:

- "I am in charge of my own life."
- "I am abundant."
- "I am successful."
- "I am empowered."
- "I am strong and beautiful."
- "I am enough."

Coaching Exercise: Think of one challenge you are currently having and coach yourself by answering the following questions. Notice how you feel.

Selfscription® Coaching Model:

What do I want?

_____

_____

_____

_____

How do I want to feel?

_____

_____

_____

_____

What obstacles are in my way?

_____

_____

_____

_____

What's my next step?

_____

_____

_____

_____

Reflections

Journal:

_____

_____

_____

_____

_____

_____

_____

_____

_____

_____

_____

_____

_____

_____

_____

_____

_____

_____

_____

_____

_____

_____

_____

_____

_____

_____

_____

_____

_____

_____

_____

_____

_____

_____

_____

Doodles:

DAY 4

Life System

Notes from Yourself:

Every area of your life is connected.
You can't focus on one area without
impacting the others.

Love,
Yourself

Happy Warrior: The Life System outlined below illustrates how each area of your life impacts every other area.

The Life System

Life is a system ... "a set of connected parts forming a complex whole." You have your own Life System, as does every other individual person, family, group, and organization (such as a business, a club, a government, etc.). When one part of a system changes, everything changes—even the smallest cog can impact the functioning of an entire system.

If you want to change a relationship with someone or make a change in another area of your life, begin with one small, manageable shift at a time. Change what you have the most control over ... Your system and your SELF. Your mind and consciousness are the operating system of your Life System. Keep those balanced, and your life will be balanced. Just be willing—willing to Let Go of old habits and willing to learn new ways of seeing and doing. If you shift, every relationship in your system shifts... You have all the power.

Happy Warrior: This exercise helps you to start breaking your life into areas and gives you a sense of where you are in each.

Life System Exercise

Look at the diagram below. Think of one area of your life in which you would like to make a change. What's one small mindset shift that you could make to move that area in the desired direction? Write your response in your notes.

Reflections

Journal:

Doodles:

KNOW THYSELF

DAY 5

Who Are You?

Notes from Yourself:

You are whoever you say you are.
Be a badass.

Love,
Yourself

Happy Warrior: Take a moment to read over the explanations below in order to better understand all areas of your life.

Who Are You?

Body: Your body is the physical vessel that carries you through life. It's quite possibly the most important area of your Life System because without the body, none of the other areas are possible. If you are investing time and energy in keeping your body healthy and happy, then it becomes far easier to show up for the other areas of your life in a positive, productive way.

Work: Your work is what you do in the world to contribute to the greater whole. Because most of us spend so much time at work, it is an important area to invest in. If you are not happy at work, that inevitably impacts every other life area. Your work also generates an income, which is another form of energy to help you provide security for yourself and your loved ones.

Money: Money is a form of energy that flows in and out of your life. Typically, you earn money from your work and spend money as a means to live and thrive and as a way to plan for the future. Money is meant to enhance, not to control, your life. It is one form of energetic currency. Mastering your money can lead to immense freedom to master the rest of your life.

Partner: Your partner is the person who travels with you through life, like your own personal co-pilot. Your partner is the person you count on and whom you also support. The most important partner you can have in life is yourself. By being a great partner to yourself, you lay the foundation for a great partner in someone else.

Connection: Connection is how you relate to and interact with all the other people in your life. That includes family, friends, coworkers, clients, acquaintances, even the person who cuts your lawn, makes you a coffee, or does your dry cleaning. How are you connecting? And what types of people do you find yourself connecting to?

Style: Style is the outward expression of how you present yourself. You are constantly surrounded by your style choices (such as the style you express in your clothing and in your home). Though often underestimated, style is an area that impacts how you feel in the world. It represents your core values and what matters most to you.

Inspiration: Inspiration is a source of energy you gain by detaching from daily responsibilities and to-do lists and allowing yourself to explore. Inspiration can be fun, playful, relaxing, peaceful, and healing—and it should be viewed as a necessary part of self-care. Without taking the time for inspiration, you can't possibly be as present and productive as you would like to be.

Happy Warrior: Now that you understand all areas of your life better, answer the questions below to determine your relationship with each of these areas.

Question: What is your current identity?

Who Are You (Now)?

Describe your relationship with each of the areas of your life. This is your current identity. Rate each area with a number from 1–10: 1 being totally unsatisfied and 10 being totally satisfied.

Body: _____

_____

Work: _____

_____

Money: _____

_____

Partner: _____

_____

Connection:_____

_____

Style: _____

_____

Inspiration: _____

_____

Happy Warrior: Now that you have established an idea of your current identity, answer the questions below to determine who it is you would like to grow into.

Question: What is your identity when you are at your best?

Who Are You (At Your Best)?

Now that you know who you are, think about whom you would like to be. In each area of your life, describe who you are, or would like to be, when you're at your best. This will give you an idea of who and what you're working towards.

Body: _____

_____

Work: _____

_____

Money: _____

_____

Partner: _____

_____

Connection:_____

_____

Style: _____

_____

Inspiration: _____

_____

Reflections

Journal:

Doodles:

DAY 6

Superpowers & Weaknesses

Notes from Yourself:

Every strength is a weakness.
Every weakness is a strength.
They are one and the same.

Love,
Yourself

Happy Warrior: Think about the characteristics that help you in your life and the ones that hold you back.

Question: What are your Superpowers and your Weaknesses?

Superpowers & Weaknesses

We're all unique, we each have a "special sauce" that makes us who we are. That special sauce contains character attributes (Superpowers) that help you shine and excel, as well as character flaws (Weaknesses) that get in the way of you being your best. Superpowers are the characteristics you feel good about, which keep you open and help you move toward your goals. Weaknesses are the characteristics that may sometimes hinder your progress and drain your energy.

Take some time to reflect on who you are. Write out your Superpowers & Weaknesses below.

1. Superpowers

_____
_____
_____
_____
_____
_____

2. Weaknesses

_____
_____
_____
_____
_____
_____

Question: How can you detach from your Superpowers & Weaknesses?

Superpowers & Weaknesses

Knowing your Superpowers and Weaknesses is an important part of knowing who you are. The catch is that every superpower can also be a weakness and every weakness can also be a superpower. They are two sides of the same coin. The key to living life as a Happy Warrior is finding the balance between them, by not building your identity or sense of self around any one of them.

Choose your top superpower and identify when it might be negatively impacting your life (making it a weakness). Choose your top weakness and identify when it might be positively impacting your life (making it a superpower).

For example, perfectionism may be a superpower because it helps you to maintain excellence in your work, but it may also be a weakness because it can paralyze you and incite you to be too hard on yourself.

1. Top Superpower to Weakness:

_____

_____

_____

_____

2. Top Weakness to Superpower:

_____

_____

_____

_____

Reflections

Journal:

_____

_____

_____

_____

_____

_____

_____

_____

_____

_____

_____

_____

_____

_____

_____

_____

_____

_____

_____

_____

_____

_____

_____

_____

_____

_____

_____

_____

_____

_____

_____

_____

_____

_____

_____

_____

_____

_____

Doodles:

DAY 7

Core Values

Notes from Yourself:

What makes you tick?
What's your "true north"?

Love,
Yourself

Happy Warrior: This exercise is about better understanding your character and how you operate.

Question: What's your "true north"? What makes you tick?

Core Values

Knowing who you are and what makes you tick are more than labels that describe what you do, how much money you make, where you live, or whether you are a man, woman, brother, sister, spouse, or parent. Who you are is determined in large part by your Core Values, which inform how you navigate relationships and situations. Use the Core Values list on the right to circle the values that are most important to you. Once you have done that, go back through your list and number your Top 5 Core Values in order of importance.

Top 5 Core Values:

List and define what each of these values mean for you, then mark each with a number from 1–10: 1 meaning you aren't living this value at all at this time, and 10 meaning you are doing your best to live this value all the time.

1. _____ – _____

_____

2. _____ – _____

_____

3. _____ – _____

_____

4. _____ – _____

_____

5. _____ – _____

_____

Happy Warrior: It can be hard to whittle it down to five, but that's okay! Give it a shot. You can always change them later.

Question: Don't see a core value you like? Add your own in the spaces provided.

Core Values

Adventure
Authenticity
Beauty
Challenge
Communication
Community
Competition
Courage
Creativity
Curiosity
Decisiveness
Dependability
Determination
Discipline
Diversity
Elegance
Empowerment
Equality
Excellence
Family
Fairness
Faith
Flexibility
Friendship
Freedom
Fun

Generosity
Growth
Happiness
Harmony
Health
Honesty
Hope
Humility
Humor
Independence
Innovation
Integrity
Intelligence
Intuition
Kindness
Love
Learning
Loyalty
Nurturing
Open-
mindedness
Order
Partnership
Patience
Peace
Perseverance

Power
Privacy
Productivity
Purpose
Recognition
Respect
Responsibility
Risk-taking
Romance
Security
Self-expression
Service to others
Spirituality
Stability
Strength
Success
Support
Teamwork
Tradition
Truth
Uniqueness
Validation
Variety
Vulnerability
Wealth
Wisdom

_____   _____   _____

Reflections

Journal:

Doodles:

DAY 8

Intuition

Notes from Yourself:

There's a wise little voice inside.
Trust it.

Love,
Yourself

Happy Warrior: We hear people talk about Intuition, but it can take some work to develop.

Question: What is that inner voice trying to tell you?

Intuition

Intuition is the practice of listening to your instincts and "gut" in order to make more conscious decisions. Your Intuition is a strong inner sense that can be even more helpful to you than your mind. The problem is, many people have ignored that inner sense so often, they can barely identify it. The amazing thing is that you can build it up again, like a muscle. It just requires practice.

In past situations that have gone awry, you probably had "a gut feeling" or a red flag early on that something just didn't "feel" right. But, because feelings are labeled irrational, unpredictable, and not based in logic, we've been programmed not to trust any of them. Your "gut feelings" are different; they are actually guiding you.

Just Ask. You always have access to your Intuition, but you have to make the decision to ask questions and tap into it.

Force vs. Allow. Forcing a particular outcome to happen can work against your instincts, whereas allowing a particular outcome to unfold means that the process feels fluid and "right."

What's the Message? When you find yourself hitting a wall, what might this difficult situation be trying to tell you?

Intuition...
Trust Yourself.
What "Feels" Right?

Happy Warrior: Now that you have a better understanding of how Intuition works, put it into practice.

Question: What am I feeling right now?

Intuition

Check in with yourself, and with your gut. Begin a practice of asking yourself, "What feels right?"

Write down one situation in which you ignored your Intuition. What happened? What did it feel like? What actions did you take? What would you have done differently if you had listened to your Intuition?

Reflections

Journal:

Doodles:

THE WAKE-UP

DAY 9

Energy

Notes from Yourself:

Everything is Energy.
Use it wisely.

Love,
Yourself

Happy Warrior: Now that we've talked about thoughts...Let's explore how different thoughts and actions can either drain or increase your Energy.

Question: How much calm, steady Energy do you feel each day?

Energy

You can choose how to manage your Energy. Building and maintaining sufficient Energy is integral to elevating your consciousness, achieving your goals, and taking your life to the next level.

Energy is the fuel that makes your Life System flow, but not all Energy is created equal. For example, the Energy that you get from sleep is better than the Energy you get from caffeine. You want the purest Energy possible to optimize your life. You want to be using the high-octane stuff!

The first step is to create an awareness of how and where you use Energy, both internally and externally, and how and where you can get more.

Internally, you drain your Energy each time you engage in self-limiting thoughts, habits, and beliefs. Externally, you drain your Energy each time you invest time and resources in people and experiences which do not give you an equal return on your Energy investment.

Replenishing your Energy, both internally and externally, is a result of engaging in productive, healthy, self-loving thoughts, actions, and habits.

On the next page, write down some of the ways in which you drain and supply your Energy. This gives you a snapshot of how your Life System is currently operating, along with some possible opportunities for growth.

Happy Warrior: The Energy exercise is an opportunity for you to drill down and see how different thoughts and actions can either drain or increase your Energy.

Question: What are you spending your Energy on?

Energy

What are your top two Energy Drains?

Internal: (e.g. "I am not enough." "I don't have enough…")
1. _____
2. _____

External: (e.g. disorganization, procrastination, taking on too much, etc.)
1. _____
2. _____

What are your top two Energy Suppliers?

Internal: Gratitude/Affirmations (e.g. "I love myself." "Good job!")
1. _____
2. _____

External: (e.g. sleep, exercise, daily planning, etc.)
1. _____
2. _____

Based on the Energy snapshot above, where can you get more Energy?
1. _____
2. _____

Reflections

Journal:

_____

_____

_____

_____

_____

_____

_____

_____

_____

_____

_____

_____

_____

_____

_____

_____

_____

_____

_____

_____

_____

_____

_____

_____

_____

_____

_____

_____

_____

_____

_____

_____

Doodles:

DAY 10

Choices & R.O.I.

Notes from Yourself:

Saying "yes" to one thing,
means saying "no" to something else.

Love,
Yourself

Happy Warrior: Evaluating your Choices & R.O.I. enables you to see how your choices have rewards and consequences.

Question: What are you saying "yes" to? What are you saying "no" to?

Choices & R.O.I. (Return on Investment)

Referring back to the Energy Exercise, building and maintaining Energy is key to achieving your goals, and this requires making choices that give you a positive return on your Energy investment. Hint: Not making a choice is a choice as well.

When you make choices that are in alignment with your Core Values and Intentions, you will see a positive return on the time and Energy you invested in those choices. This is your Return on Investment (R.O.I.).

The focus here is to be aware of the choices you are making (or not making) and how those choices impact you and the other areas of your life. The added benefit of making good choices in one life area is that they will positively impact every other area of your life.

What thoughts are you choosing on a daily basis? With whom are you are choosing to spend time? What activities are you choosing to engage in? What is the R.O.I. on each of these?

If you want to take your game up a notch, you will need to make choices that elevate your Energy levels and move you toward your goals.

Happy Warrior: The Choices & R.O.I. exercise shows you that you have more control over your Energy than you may think.

Question: What choices do you make regularly (daily/weekly) that drain your Energy?

Choices & R.O.I.

Saying "yes" to one thing means saying "no" to another. What are you saying "yes" to? What are you saying "no" to? How do these choices impact your Energy? What is the return on your investment?

For example, imagine that your best friend asks you to join them for a night out on the town, but you have set a goal to save money for a new car and a night out exceeds your current budget. If you choose to go out anyway, what will you be saying "yes" to? You are saying "yes" to investing Energy in your friendship. What might you be saying "no" to? Having a new car by a certain date.

Every choice impacts the entire system. The most important thing is that you are aware of your choices and that ultimately, you are doing what will bring you the most happiness in the long term.

What have you said "yes" to that gave you a positive R.O.I.?

_____

_____

What have you said "yes" to that gave you a negative R.O.I.?

_____

_____

Reflections

Journal:

Doodles:

DAY 11

The Life of a Feeling

Notes from Yourself:

Feelings are temporary.
Let them pass through you.

Love,
Yourself

Happy Warrior: The Life of a Feeling is an opportunity for you to see feelings as something separate from your identity (e.g. "I feel angry" vs. "I am angry"). Awareness is key, but we will all have great days and tough days—such is life.

Question: Which feelings do you identify with most often?

The Life of a Feeling

Feelings are temporary. Whether positive or negative, they are not meant to take up permanent residence in your body or your life. When you attach to any type of feeling, you could end up strengthening a false story or creating a self-limiting belief about life, love, or yourself. The only way to counteract this destructive process is by learning to allow your feelings to pass on through.

The Life of a Feeling is the trajectory of a feeling from beginning to end. Notice the feeling, name it, feel it, celebrate it, cry about it, talk about it, write about it. Then, take a step back and just observe, without judgment, and let it go. This is a huge step toward elevating both your consciousness and your emotional intelligence.

Let's say you have just suffered a breakup and you feel a lot of sadness, anger, or resentment. This means that you will probably tell people that you ARE sad, or that you ARE angry. But the truth is, you are EXPERIENCING sadness and you are EXPERIENCING anger. Your job is to prevent these feelings from sticking around and creating false stories like, "I'll never find anybody," or "there are no good partners out there," or "I have failed." Sadness and anger are just feelings—they will fade, if you allow them to.

Happy Warrior: The Life of a Feeling exercise sets the stage to "Explore: The Feelings," which we will cover later. A great day is an "open" day and a tough day is a "closed" day.

Question: How does a great day feel? How does a tough day feel?

The Life of a Feeling

The Life of a Feeling is about not attaching to the feeling and instead, allowing it to pass through you. Whatever you are feeling now is going to change. You are going to feel differently at some point.

Describe a great day you have had. How did you feel? Do you still feel that way today?

_____

_____

_____

_____

_____

_____

_____

_____

Describe a tough day you have had. How did you feel? Do you still feel that way today?

_____

_____

_____

_____

_____

_____

_____

_____

Reflections

Journal:

Doodles:

DAY 12

You Are Not Your Thoughts

Notes from Yourself:

You Are Not Your Thoughts;
you are the observer of your thoughts.

Love,
Yourself

Happy Warrior: One of our main sources of suffering lies in our attachment to our thoughts. By recognizing that You Are Not Your Thoughts, but actually the observer of your thoughts, you take a critical step in freeing your mind.

You Are Not Your Thoughts

Ninety percent of what you think today you already thought yesterday. At any given moment, your mind is likely filled with an endless stream of thoughts. The most critical component to harnessing your Energy and Elevating Your Consciousness is realizing that you are not your inner dialogue; you are the observer of that dialogue. Under all the thoughts and feelings lies the wisest, most complete version of yourself—and it is your job to uncover it.

Your mind is meant to be used as a tool to help you function in the world. Unfortunately, at some point, you stopped using your mind as a tool and it started using you. If you are like everyone else in the world, you are dominated by your thoughts, feelings, and false stories every day. Your connection to your thoughts is like an abusive co-dependent relationship— you are allowing yourself to be abused, all day every day.

It's time to take your power back. Whether you are in the car or at the grocery store or your office, you can simply notice your inner dialogue: "Oh, there it is again." This is how you learn to start managing your thoughts and detach from those thoughts that don't serve you, giving yourself space for beautiful, new, empowering thoughts to arise. These are the thoughts that will help you Take Your Life to the Next Level.

Happy Warrior: The exercise below helps you to see the impact of your thoughts on your life, and how simply changing those thoughts will change your life.

You Are Not Your Thoughts

Be an Observer.

Observe your thoughts. Do you notice any repetition in what you are thinking about from one day to the next? Write down some of these thoughts below:

How do you feel as a result of these thoughts?

How would you feel without these thoughts?
Free Your Mind…

Reflections

Journal:

Doodles:

DAY 13

Triggers & Lack Loops

Notes from Yourself:

Are you on a mental hamster wheel?
What keeps it spinning?

Love,
Yourself

Happy Warrior: We all have old wounds that flare up and cause us new grief. We can't heal them if we don't know what they are.

Question: Which Triggers send you into a Lack Loop?

Triggers & Lack Loops

What is a Trigger? A Trigger is a negative emotional reaction inside of you, causing you to close down. It happens in real time, with current people and experiences, but it originates from old wounds, past disappointments, or compromised values. Triggers activate the oldest part of your brain, known as the "reptilian brain," and are experienced as emotional disruptions that create closed physical sensations in your body. Your heart might race, your palms might sweat, or you may feel nervous or anxious. Equally, you might feel compelled to run away or to fight to protect yourself, or you may feel totally paralyzed.

What is a Lack Loop? Triggers unleash a repetitive pattern of connections in your brain. What this means is that you can find yourself repeating the same lack-based stories and feelings over and over. Maybe you replay what someone said or did or what you would like to have said or done, over and over. Each time you are Triggered and find yourself replaying things that make you feel angry, sad, or upset, you are in a Lack Loop. The outward reflection of this loop may include irritation, frustration, anger, blame, shutting down, and many of the physical sensations listed above. These are all Energy drains, which are keeping you closed and stuck in an unproductive cycle.

When you feel Triggered, it is an opportunity to Let Go of that old story or wound and heal the painful imprint left by past experiences. You have a choice. By developing a practice of awareness around your Triggers, you will have the power to break your Lack Loops. With the use of S.E.L.F. you will have the tools to pioneer a whole new path to Elevate Your Consciousness and Free Your Mind.

Happy Warrior: Now that you better understand Triggers & Lack Loops, it is time to dig into yours so you can heal them!

Question: What irritates you? How does that feel in your body?

Triggers

What Triggers you? In other words, in what instances do you feel angry, impatient, sad, or shut down? For example, perhaps you get Triggered when you are not feeling heard, respected, or valued. Or, you may get Triggered when someone is late for a meeting or doesn't respond to your call or email. Do any of these things Trigger a closed emotional response? Can you think of any other examples of being Triggered? List them below:

_____

_____

_____

_____

_____

_____

_____

Now that you know some of your Triggers, which physical sensations do you feel in your body when you are Triggered? List them below. (Hint: physical sensations can also indicate Triggers you may not be aware of.)

_____

_____

_____

_____

_____

_____

Reflections

Journal:

_____

_____

_____

_____

_____

_____

_____

_____

_____

_____

_____

_____

_____

_____

_____

_____

_____

_____

_____

_____

_____

_____

_____

_____

_____

_____

_____

_____

_____

_____

_____

_____

_____

_____

_____

_____

Doodles:

DAY 14

The Power of Affirmations

Notes from Yourself:

You have the power to shift your mindset.
Shift your thoughts; change your life.

Love,
Yourself

Happy Warrior: Using Affirmations is a powerful way for you to coach yourself, shift your mindset, and live a more empowered life.

The Power of Affirmations

Affirmations are one of the most important ways to keep your thoughts and life moving forward.

Affirmations Elevate Your Consciousness by helping you to:

- affirm and validate yourself, especially when the going gets tough (e.g. affirming, "I am perfectly imperfect, just as I am")
- keep your eyes on the prize
- stay open to everything life has to offer

Most of us spend plenty of time "beating ourselves up" (or even "beating up" other people) by indulging in false stories and self-limiting beliefs. Plenty of books on motivation and productivity will tell you that negative reinforcement is not always the most effective method to attain success. Using Affirmations provides a much more productive path.

Have you ever been to a bowling alley? You can add bumpers to the gutters so that regardless of your skill level, the ball will stay in your lane—and hopefully hit a couple of pins. In the same way, using Affirmations keeps your thoughts and Energy out of the gutter, on track, and focused on what you want.

You can be your own worst enemy, but by keeping your mind out of the gutter, you can become your own biggest advocate.

Happy Warrior: The Power of Affirmations exercise gives you an opportunity to walk through the process of writing an Affirmation so that, ultimately, you can create your own Affirmations for any life challenge.

The Power of Affirmations

How to write an Affirmation:

- Know what you want or how you want to feel.
- Believe that you can have it, be it, and feel it.
- Write it in the present tense.

For example:

- I have the power to achieve my goals.
- I am taking my life to the next level.
- I am elevating my consciousness.
- I am powerful.
- I am worthy.
- I am enough.

Reflections

Journal:

Doodles:

MIDPOINT CHECK-IN

Happy Warrior: The Mid-Point provides you with a snapshot of the progress you have made so far.

Mid-Point

On a scale of 1–10, how happy are you right now?

_____

_____

What shifts in your perspective do you feel good about since you started your journey?

_____

_____

What tangible accomplishments do you feel good about since your first session?

_____

_____

What percentage of your time do you spend being open vs. being closed to yourself and to what life has to offer?

_____

_____

What is working well on this happiness journey?

_____

_____

_____

What additional support might you need?

_____

_____

_____

S.E.L.F.

DAY 15

Stop: Breathe

Notes from Yourself:

*Find the stillness behind your thoughts,
and watch the answers bubble up.*

Love,
Yourself

Happy Warrior: Stop: Breathe is the first step toward becoming an empowered Happy Warrior.

Stop: Breathe

Stop: Breathe is the foundation for elevating your consciousness and taking your life to the next level. When you do the Stop: Breathe exercise, you are choosing to take a step back and:

- Observe your thoughts
- Manage your Energy
- Make conscious choices
- Create space for clarity and stillness

Exercise

Stop: Breathe is the most impactful practice you can integrate into your daily life. At any moment, you have the choice to Stop whatever you are doing and whatever you are thinking to take a breath and detach from your inner dialogue.

Spend the upcoming weeks simply noticing what's happening inside of you. Throughout the day, pause occasionally, create a moment of stillness, and allow yourself to not think. Keep a running tally of how many times you are able to Stop: Breathe and note how that felt. Did any shifts occur? Did you come to any moments of clarity? Note your observations on your Reflections page.

Happy Warrior: Nobody can be an empowered Happy Warrior without Meditation & Mindfulness. Read the writeup below and commit to a time and place to meditate each day.

Meditation & Mindfulness

Meditation is simply Stop: Breathe, and is the foundation for sharpening your mind. Meditation allows you to detach from endless internal dialogue and establish a reference point for inner peace. Meditation is a time-out, a moment to get grounded and connect with yourself. It reduces stress, enhances focus, and even helps you sleep. The key to meditation is consistency.

Mindfulness is the art of being aware. It is the art of being present instead of rehashing the past or worrying about the future. By practicing Mindfulness throughout the day, you can assess whether you are using your Energy to stay stuck in a problem or to move into a solution. Being mindful enables you to harness your Energy and Elevate Your Consciousness.

Meditation and Mindfulness go hand-in-hand. With a consistent daily meditation practice, you will be more mindful throughout the rest of your day. You will find opportunities to Stop, Explore, Let Go, and Free Your Mind.

Want to go deeper?

Find a time and place to meditate for a minimum of five total minutes each day (which can be thirty seconds in one place and sixty seconds in another). Keep a meditation log, record how long you sat still, and note any internal shifts you notice.

Reflections

Journal:

Doodles:

DAY 16

Explore the Feelings & False Stories

Notes from Yourself:

Don't believe everything you tell yourself.
Not all thoughts are created equal.

Love,
Yourself

Happy Warrior: Being an empowered Happy Warrior requires you to be mindful of whether you are Open or Closed in any given moment.

Question: Are you Open or Closed?

Explore: The Feelings

Are you Open or Closed to what life has to offer? When you are Open, your thoughts are operating from a calm, centered, loving place. When you are Closed O.F.F. (Operating from Fear) your thoughts are operating from an anxious, fearful, stressed, or frustrated place.

If you take a moment to recall what it feels like to be happy, confident, and fulfilled, you will realize how Open and expansive that feels. On the other hand, if you take a moment to recall what it feels like to be stressed, irritable, or afraid, you will realize how Closed and restricted that feels. (A visual example is to think of an open palm versus a closed fist.)

If you are going through life with an Open palm, you are successfully managing your thoughts and feelings, you listen to your Intuition, and you are open to solutions and opportunities. If you are going through life with a Closed fist, you are investing your Energy in fear-based thoughts and problems, and you are Closed O.F.F. to your internal compass and the opportunities around you.

The S.E.L.F. process gives you the necessary tools to help you remain Open, so you can flow through life fluidly with more joy, fulfillment, and success.

Happy Warrior: In the exercise below, you can start to gain more awareness of which feelings are Open and which are Closed.

Question: Are you Open or Closed?

Explore: The Feelings

Using the lists below as a guide, make a habit of identifying when you are Open vs. Closed.

Open Self: (Love-Based):	Closed Self: (Fear-Based):
• Happy	• Angry
• Confident	• Irritated
• Joyous	• Annoyed
• Grateful	• Frustrated
• Excited	• Impatient
• Alive	• Disempowered
• Sexy	• Small
• Passionate	• Upset
• Inspired	• Hurt
• Relaxed	• Anxious
• Hopeful	• Blaming
• Awed	• Worried
• Tender	• Confused
• Caring	• Ashamed
• Compassionate	• Guilty
• Loving	• Embarrassed
• Capable	• Nervous
• Empowered	• Numb
• Eager	• Empty
• Peaceful	• Sad
• Humble	• Jealous
• Silly	• Lonely
• Light	• Lacking
• Liberated	• Disappointed
• Free	• Overwhelmed
• Brave	• Stressed
• Blessed	• Depressed
• Complete	• Judgemental

Happy Warrior: Many of your negative or "closed" feelings are fueled by old "false" stories that are living in your belief system. They may have protected you at one time but are no longer helping you.

Question: What are your false stories?

Explore: The False Stories

What are you thinking?

Every day, your thoughts and feelings are running incessantly through your mind and body, becoming part of your identity. This incessant chatter is preventing you from being present and engaged in your life. By making a practice out of observing your thoughts and feelings, you start to slowly detach from them; this allows you to be more present and to become more aware. In doing so, you also start to trace some of these recurring thoughts and emotions back to False Stories.

What are your False Stories?

All of your experiences inform who you are, and some of them have led you to develop certain self-limiting rules or beliefs about life, other people, and yourself. These beliefs are called "False Stories." Once a False Story has been formed (e.g. "I'm not good enough" or "people can't be trusted"), you begin to hardwire these stories into your identity. Each time you confront a circumstance that Triggers a False Story, you find yourself filled with Closed emotions such as anger, shame, blame, guilt, or sadness, which can leave you feeling drained.

Happy Warrior: Take time to recognize and understand your own False Stories, so you can acknowledge and manage them when they present themselves.

Question: What are your False Stories?

Explore: The False Stories

How do you know when you are running a False Story?
- You're feeling angry, stressed, frustrated, etc.
- You're experiencing not having/being enough
- You're judging yourself and/or others
- You're taking something personally
- You're comparing yourself to others
- You're Closed O.F.F. – Operating from Fear
- You're beating yourself up

Examples of False Stories:
- "I'm not good enough."
- "I'm not ____ enough (rich, smart, good-looking, skinny…)."
- "I'm too____ (old, fat, stupid…)."
- "Other people are____ (old, fat, stupid…)."
- "I will never find love because…."
- "I can't relate to others because…."
- "I'm terrible at spelling, technology, yoga…."
- "People suck and are untrustworthy."
- "There are no good men/women in ____ (name of city)."
- "I don't have the "right" degree" or background."
- "I'm an imposter. People will find out."
- "I'm a failure."
- "I'm not as good as others."
- "I'm better than others."
- "I'm invisible and I don't matter."
- "People won't like me if…."
- "I don't like other people because…."

Happy Warrior: Take time to recognize and understand your own False Stories, so you can acknowledge and manage them when they present themselves.

Question: What are your False Stories?

Explore: The False Stories

Identify and write out the top False Stories that hold you back, along with the accompanying feelings.

Reflections

Journal:

Doodles:

DAY 17

Let Go

Notes from Yourself:

You're the author of your life.
Write your own story.

Love,
Yourself

Happy Warrior: You have already looked at the things in your life you need to Let Go of. Now, it is time to look internally at the thoughts and feelings that are no longer serving you.

Question: What thoughts and feelings can you Let Go of?

Let Go

This internal approach to Letting Go is about releasing the Energy that no longer serves you and giving yourself permission to be where you are right now … by affirming that You Are Enough.

Throughout your life, you have developed certain protective defenses in order to navigate difficult situations. Those were needed and served you well at times. As you have grown, your circumstances have changed, but the protective defenses have remained, and have become an unneeded weight, holding you back.

These old feelings became False Stories you are still carrying around. You are probably experiencing heaviness or Triggers, reminding you that they are still there and need to be released.

Now, it is time to let them go by catching them in the moment:

- Stop: Breathe
- Explore: The Feelings and False Stories
- Let Go….

By rewriting your False Stories to affirm that You Are Enough, you chip away at your old self-limiting beliefs and create space for a new, empowering identity to shine through.

Happy Warrior: Rewriting your False Stories is one of the most empowering practices of a Happy Warrior. Let Go of old stagnant beliefs and empower yourself to start over.

Question: What thoughts and feelings can you Let Go of?

Let Go

Rewrite your false stories in order to Let Go and give yourself permission to be enough right now (e.g. "I am abundant." "I am empowered." "I am perfectly imperfect.").

_____
_____
_____
_____
_____

_____
_____
_____
_____

_____
_____
_____
_____

_____
_____
_____
_____

_____
_____
_____
_____

Happy Warrior: Certain beliefs and grievances are deep and harder to Let Go of. If you have any of those, take time out. Write a letter to yourself or to someone else, which will enable you to heal and move forward. (Hint: you don't have to send the letter.)

Question: What thoughts and feelings can you Let Go of?

Let Go

Writing a Letter of Forgiveness

There are some situations and False Stories that run deeper and require more work for you to Let Go of them. One way to approach this is by writing a letter of forgiveness. A forgiveness letter allows you to describe the hurt in detail: how it felt at the time and how you feel about it now. You can also share any residual hurt, guilt, disappointment, anger, or shame you may still be experiencing. Then, you can make the conscious choice to let it all go, so that it no longer has power to hurt you or define you. Later, you may even start to ask yourself what you learned from the experience and how it made you a better person. You don't need to send your forgiveness letter to anyone. It is for your eyes only—and for your own self-empowerment. Using the space below, list anyone you may need to forgive or ask for forgiveness. At your own pace, and in your own way, write your letters of forgiveness in the journal of your choice.

Reflections

Journal:

_____
_____
_____
_____
_____
_____
_____
_____
_____
_____
_____
_____
_____
_____
_____
_____
_____
_____
_____
_____
_____
_____
_____
_____
_____
_____
_____
_____
_____
_____

Doodles:

DAY 18

Free Your Mind & S.E.L.F.

Notes from Yourself:

*Free Your Mind,
and the rest will follow.*

Love,
Yourself

Happy Warrior: Now that you are breathing, exploring your feelings, and letting go, you will find you have more space and Energy to focus on what matters most to you.

Question: How can you remember to use S.E.L.F.?

Free Your Mind

> *"Unencumber yourself from the regrets of the past and worries of the future."*
> —Selfscription®

"Free Your Mind" is the last step of S.E.L.F. It is the exhalation and the reward for raising your awareness and choosing to be Open vs. Closed.

"Free Your Mind" is the intention you have been working toward. Every time you Stop: Breathe; Explore: The Feelings and The False Stories; and Let Go, you are creating space in your mind and your life to be Open, make conscious choices, and Take Your Life to the Next Level.

The good news is that nothing actually needs to change—except you choosing to release the Triggers and stories that have been on auto-replay. The S.E.L.F. process is about managing the inner dialogue and stepping off your inner soapbox in order to Free Your Mind and lay the foundation for a life of confidence, productivity, and fulfillment.

Happy Warrior: It's time to put it all together.

Question: Are you feeling lighter? How about freer?

S. E. L. F.

S.E.L.F. is the process of opening yourself up, creating awareness about who you are now, and shifting your perspective to become more of who you want to be.

You have now learned the four steps of S.E.L.F. By employing these steps, you slowly begin to dismantle the old identification with your Triggers, Lack Loops, False Stories, and self-limiting beliefs. Each time you work through the S.E.L.F. process, you are creating new, more open, and energizing pathways to Elevate Your Consciousness and Free Your Mind.

Let's create the S.E.L.F. habit. Choose a time and add a daily reminder to your phone or computer to use the entire S.E.L.F. process. By making S.E.L.F. into a habit, you will have tools at your disposal whenever you need to reenergize, refocus, and move through anything holding you back.

S. E. L. F.:

- Stop: Breathe.
- Explore: What are the Feelings and False stories?
- Let Go: Affirm You Are Enough.
- Free Your Mind…..

Reflections

Journal:

Doodles:

READY, SET, GO!

DAY 19

Create Space

Notes from Yourself:

*Let Go of what no longer works;
create space for what does.*

Love,
Yourself

Happy Warrior: Creating space is a vital part of your ability to grow. Just like a plant may need to drop leaves, you have to make space in your life for new growth by letting go of what no longer works.

Question: What can you Let Go of in order to create space?

Create Space

A large part of elevating your consciousness is about learning to Let Go. In the S.E.L.F. section, we discuss Letting Go of thoughts and feelings that no longer serve you, but there's also an external component to Letting Go. Letting Go is not only about releasing what's no longer working; it's also about creating space for what does work.

If you look in your closet or around your home and see things you haven't worn or used in a long time, there are probably other parts of your life in which you are holding onto something that no longer works. Should you throw out those threadbare socks or the old saggy underwear before buying new ones? Yes, because you need to make room for the socks, underwear, and all the things that you actually DO want. This requires trust.

A huge part of letting go is trusting that you are going to get what you need on the other end. The only way you can do this is to practice letting go. What you will find is that time and time again you end up with a better partner, a better job, and even better underwear. In fact, letting go of the old stuff leaves you wide open and ready to embrace something new and more fulfilling. So, assess what you might need to Let Go of—and get ready to liberate yourself.

Happy Warrior: Now, take a moment to think about some things that are no longer serving you. By letting these go, you can create space for more of what does serve you.

Question: What can you Let Go of in order to create space?

Create Space

What are some things that you need to Let Go of?

List some external things you need to Let Go of. For example, do you have a pile of old magazines that you haven't touched in a while and probably never will again? Or do you have a stack of mail that needs to be sorted...or some old, crusty travel-sized shampoo bottles under the sink?

Let Go of one of these things. Release the stagnant Energy and open yourself up.

Keep going. If you have more to purge, make a plan to purge one thing per day for the remainder of this journey and beyond. Even if it is just a pair of socks you no longer love...let them go.

Reflections

Journal:

Doodles:

DAY 20

Daily Rituals & Planning

Notes from Yourself:

*Rituals are the anchors that keep
your life from floating away.*

Love,
Yourself

Happy Warrior: Daily Rituals are the practices that keep you grounded and detached from your thoughts on a day-to-day basis, so that you have a platform to push off of in order to move forward.

Question: What daily rituals ground you?

Daily Rituals

Daily Rituals are anchor habits that ground you in your commitment to yourself. When you start each morning by giving yourself time to meditate, exercise, journal, pray, or read inspirational literature, you are starting each day by prioritizing yourself. Give yourself time each morning to not be plugged into the outside world through a phone or computer.

Equally, when you wind down each evening by planning the next day and practicing gratitude, you are completing your day by prioritizing yourself, your sleep, your centeredness, and your goals.

Choose a special space or spaces for your rituals to take place. Prepare anything you may need in advance: Reflection Journal, Pocket Planner, prayer beads, candles, books, or music. Your rituals should be easy to maintain and should make you feel amazing.

Example Morning Rituals	*Example Evening Rituals*
• Meditate	• Next Day Planning
• Journal	• Gratitude Journal
• Pray	• Lay Out Clothes
• Pack Lunch	• Read

Happy Warrior: A few ideas of rituals we like: drinking coffee, meditating, writing in a gratitude journal, planning your day (or, in the evening, planning the following day), drinking a cup of tea, praying, reading inspirational books.

Question: What rituals help you to be your best SELF?

Daily Rituals

Using the examples we've given, use the template below to outline the Morning & Evening Rituals that will help you to operate as your most open, energized, and productive self.

Morning Rituals

¤ _____

¤ _____

¤ _____

Evening Rituals

¤ _____

¤ _____

¤ _____

How would your life shift if you gave yourself the gift of "me-time" for Daily Rituals each morning and evening?

_____
_____
_____
_____
_____
_____

Reflections

Journal:

_____

_____

_____

_____

_____

_____

_____

_____

_____

_____

_____

_____

_____

_____

_____

_____

_____

_____

_____

_____

_____

_____

_____

_____

_____

_____

_____

_____

_____

_____

_____

_____

_____

Doodles:

DAY 21

5-Year Life Vision

Notes from Yourself:

Where ya goin', beautiful?
How you gonna get there?

Love,
Yourself

Happy Warrior: Having a longer-term vision gives you a "true north" to guide you through your short-term decisions.

Question: Who do you want to be in five years?

5-Year Life Vision

Happy Warrior: If you wanna get somewhere, you gotta know where it is you wanna go.

Question: What's your wildest dream?

5-Year Life Vision

Let's fast-forward five years… Imagine you run into an old friend who asks what's been happening in your life. What's your best-case scenario? What would you love to say has been happening in your life?

Write out your 5-Year Life Vision below, for each of the areas of your Life System. Have fun with it!

Body: _____
_____
_____
_____
_____
_____

Work: _____
_____
_____
_____
_____
_____

Money: _____
_____
_____
_____
_____
_____

Partner: _____

_____

_____

_____

_____

_____

_____

Connection: _____

_____

_____

_____

_____

_____

_____

Style: _____

_____

_____

_____

_____

_____

_____

Inspiration: _____

_____

_____

_____

_____

_____

Reflections

Journal:

Doodles:

DAY 22

1-Year Goals

Notes from Yourself:

*Goals are just habits
you've shown up for.*

Love,
Yourself

Happy Warrior: Goal-setting is a process and an art. Let's set some goals, along with plans for how to achieve them!

Question: What are you working toward?

Goal-Setting

Goals are the specific, achievable milestones you wish to reach by a target date, as well as the Habits & Actions necessary to achieve them. Since Goals can feel heavy or overwhelming, make them fun!

Habits

Habits are the ritual practices that you design to reach your Goals. For example, if your Goal is to find a new job, one Habit might be to set aside time every evening to review job listings and send out your resume.

Actions

Actions are one-time items that you check off as soon as they are completed. For example, if your Goal is to find a new job, one Action would be to update your resume.

Now, let's set some Goals!

On the following page, write down your 1-Year Goals, break them down into Quarterly Goals, and then transfer your Quarterly Goals to the corresponding Goal page (Body, Work, Partner, etc.). Once completed, this is where you will break the Goals down into Habits & Actions.

Happy Warrior: One of the key practices in goal-setting is creating longer-term Goals that you break down into pieces. Below, set some 1-Year Goals, which we will break into Quarters.

Question: What's your plan?

1-Year Goals

For each life area, set a 1-Year Goal that will move you toward your 5-Year Life Vision.

Body: _____

_____

Work: _____

_____

Money: _____

_____

Partner: _____

_____

Connection:_____

_____

Style: _____

_____

Inspiration: _____

_____

Reflections

Journal:

Doodles:

DAY 23

Quarterly Goals

Notes from Yourself:

*Break it down ... one
step at a time.*

Love,
Yourself

Happy Warrior: Goal-setting is a process and an art. Let's set up some Goals, along with plans for how to achieve them!

Question: What are you working toward?

Goal-Setting

Goals are the specific, achievable milestones you wish to reach by a target date, as well as the Habits & Actions necessary to achieve them. Since Goals can feel heavy or overwhelming, make them fun!

Habits

Habits are the ritual practices that you design to reach your Goals. For example, if your Goal is to find a new job, one Habit might be to set aside time every evening to review job listings and send out your resume.

Actions

Actions are one-time items that you check off as soon as they are completed. For example, if your Goal is to find a new job, one Action would be to update your resume.

Now let's set some Goals!

On the following pages, you will break down your 1-Year Goals into Quarterly Goals, transfer your Quarterly Goals to the corresponding Goal pages (Body, Work, Partner, etc.), and identify the Habits & Actions necessary to achieve these Goals.

Happy Warrior: You have your 1-Year Goals, now it is time to break them into Quarterly Goals. It's one step at a time.

Question: What is the first Quarterly Goal that will move you toward the 1-Year Goal?

Quarterly Goals

For each life area, set a Quarterly Goal that will move you toward your 1-Year Goal.

Body: _____

_____

Work: _____

_____

Money: _____

_____

Partner: _____

_____

Connection:_____

_____

Style: _____

_____

Inspiration: _____

_____

Reflections

Journal:

Doodles:

DAY 24

Goal-Setting & Body Goal

Notes from Yourself:

Your body is your vehicle.
Regular service is required.

Love,
Yourself

Example Quarterly Goals

Start Date: Jan 1, 2019
Due Date: March 31, 2019

Goal:

Find a new job. (Make it fun!)

> *Land an awesome new gig!*

What will life be like when you achieve this goal?

> *I will wake up every morning looking forward to my day. I will be working with cool, like-minded people, making a great living, and living life to the fullest.*

What must you Let Go of to achieve this goal?

> *I must Let Go of the fear of rejection and my self-limiting belief that I am not qualified for the jobs that I want.*

Habits necessary to achieve this goal:

- Daily job search and company research
- Daily follow-up on jobs to which I've applied
- Update Job-Search Spreadsheet

Actions necessary to achieve this goal:

- Update LinkedIn Profile
- Update Resume and Cover Letter
- Set up Spreadsheet, Process, and Daily Habits
- Buy New Interview Outfit

Happy Warrior: Now that you have your Quarterly Body Goal, explore it a little bit and break it down even further into the Habits & Actions you need to take to get there.

Question: How can you honor your Body?

Body Goal

Refer back to the Goals page. Take the corresponding goal from the Goals page and make it actionable.

Start Date: _____, _____, _____

Due Date: _____, _____, _____

Goal: _____

_____

What will life be like when you achieve this Goal?

_____

_____

_____

What must you Let Go of to achieve this Goal?

_____

_____

_____

Habits necessary to achieve this Goal:

▢ _____

▢ _____

▢ _____

Actions necessary to achieve this Goal:

▢ _____

▢ _____

▢ _____

Reflections

Journal:

_____

_____

_____

_____

_____

_____

_____

_____

_____

_____

_____

_____

_____

_____

_____

_____

_____

_____

_____

_____

_____

_____

_____

_____

_____

_____

_____

_____

_____

_____

Doodles:

DAY 25

Work & Money Goals

Notes from Yourself:

Focus on what you love, and happiness will follow.

Love,
Yourself

Happy Warrior: Now that you have your Quarterly Work Goal, explore it a little bit and break it down even further into the Habits & Actions you need to take to get there.

Question: What would you like to learn or accomplish?

Work Goal

Refer back to the Goals page. Take the corresponding Goal from the Goals page and make it actionable.

Start Date: _____, _____, _____
Due Date: _____, _____, _____

Goal: _____
_____

What will life be like when you achieve this Goal?
_____
_____
_____

What must you Let Go of to achieve this Goal?
_____
_____
_____

Habits necessary to achieve this Goal:
¤ _____
¤ _____
¤ _____

Actions necessary to achieve this Goal:
¤ _____
¤ _____
¤ _____

Happy Warrior: Now that you have your Quarterly Money Goal, explore it a little bit and break it down even further into the Habits & Actions you need to take to get there.

Question: How can your Money serve you?

Money Goal

Refer back to the Goals page. Take the corresponding Goal from the Goals page and make it actionable.

Start Date: _____, _____, _____
Due Date: _____, _____, _____

Goal: _____
_____

What will life be like when you achieve this Goal?
_____
_____
_____

What must you Let Go of to achieve this Goal?
_____
_____
_____

Habits necessary to achieve this Goal:
¤ _____
¤ _____
¤ _____

Actions necessary to achieve this Goal:
¤ _____
¤ _____
¤ _____

Reflections

Journal:

Doodles:

DAY 26

Partner & Connection Goals

Notes from Yourself:

Life is about learning to love yourself and others.

Love,
Yourself

Happy Warrior: Now that you have your Quarterly Partner Goal, explore it a little bit and break it down even further into the Habits & Actions you need to take to get there.

Question: Are you open and available for a Partner?

Partner Goal

Refer back to the Goals page. Take the corresponding Goal from the Goals page and make it actionable.

Start Date: _____, _____, _____
Due Date: _____, _____, _____

Goal: _____
_____

What will life be like when you achieve this Goal?
_____
_____
_____

What must you Let Go of to achieve this Goal?
_____
_____
_____

Habits necessary to achieve this Goal:
◻ _____
◻ _____
◻ _____

Actions necessary to achieve this Goal:
◻ _____
◻ _____
◻ _____

Happy Warrior: Now that you have your Quarterly Connection Goal, explore it a little bit and break it down even further into the Habits & Actions you need to take to get there.

Question: How are you and your Connections showing up for each other?

Connection Goal

Refer back to the Goals page. Take the corresponding Goal from the Goals page and make it actionable.

Start Date: _____, _____, _____
Due Date: _____, _____, _____

Goal: _____
_____

What will life be like when you achieve this Goal?
_____
_____
_____

What must you Let Go of to achieve this Goal?
_____
_____
_____

Habits necessary to achieve this Goal:
☐ _____
☐ _____
☐ _____

Actions necessary to achieve this Goal:
☐ _____
☐ _____
☐ _____

Reflections

Journal:

_____

_____

_____

_____

_____

_____

_____

_____

_____

_____

_____

_____

_____

_____

_____

_____

_____

_____

_____

_____

_____

_____

_____

_____

_____

_____

_____

_____

_____

_____

_____

_____

_____

_____

_____

_____

_____

Doodles:

DAY 27

Style & Inspiration Goals

Notes from Yourself:

*Surround yourself with beauty
and do things you love.*

Love,
Yourself

Happy Warrior: Now that you have your Quarterly Style Goal, explore it a little bit and break it down even further into the Habits & Actions you need to take to get there.

Question: Does your home or wardrobe need a makeover?

Style Goal

Refer back to the Goals page. Take the corresponding Goal from the Goals page and make it actionable.

Start Date: _____, _____, _____
Due Date: _____, _____, _____

Goal: _____
_____

What will life be like when you achieve this Goal?
_____
_____
_____

What must you Let Go of to achieve this Goal?
_____
_____
_____

Habits necessary to achieve this Goal:
☐ _____
☐ _____
☐ _____

Actions necessary to achieve this Goal:
☐ _____
☐ _____
☐ _____

Happy Warrior: Now that you have your Quarterly Inspiration Goal, explore it a little bit and break it down even further into the Habits & Actions you need to take to get there.

Question: Are you having fun?

Inspiration Goal

Refer back to the Goals page. Take the corresponding Goal from the Goals page and make it actionable.

Start Date: _____, _____, _____
Due Date: _____, _____, _____

Goal: _____
_____

What will life be like when you achieve this Goal?
_____
_____
_____

What must you Let Go of to achieve this Goal?
_____
_____
_____

Habits necessary to achieve this Goal:
¤ _____
¤ _____
¤ _____

Actions necessary to achieve this Goal:
¤ _____
¤ _____
¤ _____

Reflections

Journal:

Doodles:

WRAP IT UP

DAY 28

Live It, Share It, Celebrate It

Notes from Yourself:

If you can see it, you can be it.

Love,
Yourself

Happy Warrior: You have a plan, and now it's time to put it into action by incorporating all of these habits and actions into your life.

Question: What's the first step?

Live It, Share It, Celebrate It

We are what we consume, and we are constantly taking in the world around us, whether it is art, food, television, or people's Energy. Part of incorporating a happiness mindset and achieving the life you have always dreamed of is to have a plan of action, surround yourself with the right people, be accountable for your Goals, find ways to inspire yourself, and move step by step toward your Life Vision. Everything counts!

Live It:

Now that you have acquired the tools to shift your mindset and you have clarified the Habits & Actions you need to adopt to achieve your Goals, it is time to map out your next steps. Where many people wander off track is in trying to do too much at once. *Slow and steady wins the race*—which means that we need to pick one to two new Habits to work on at any one time. In order to successfully incorporate any new Habit into your life, you also have to think about what else needs to shift in your life to accommodate that Habit.

Share It:

One key way to help yourself achieve your Goals is to have supportive, encouraging people around you, as well as people who can hold you accountable to becoming the person you want to be. Sometimes these are the same people and sometimes they are different. But identifying who those people are is a great first step to success.

Celebrate It:

Another key factor in achieving your Goals is to not shame yourself each time you don't show up the way you think you should. Acknowledging yourself and giving yourself a win is how you foster and cultivate that new Habit in your life. Whether it is a simple, "Nice job," or it is a gift you buy yourself or a trip you take, focus on what you DID do instead of what you didn't do. That's how new Habits are formed, and that's how Goals and Visions are realized.

Happy Warrior: Visions and Goals are accomplished best when you have accountability. Share them with people you love and trust!

Question: How will you inspire and support your Goals while holding yourself accountable?

Live It, Share It, Celebrate It

First, refer back to the Goals page. Take one to two Goals you want to focus on and establish a timeline to complete them. Second, ask people in your life to support and help you and let them know what their role is. Last, give yourself a win! The only way to live the life you have dreamed of is by celebrating your successes.

Live It:

What are the one to two Habits you want to adopt? What life changes need to be made in order to successfully adopt them?

_____

_____

_____

_____

_____

Share It:

Who will support you and cheer you on? (This can also be you!)

_____

Who will hold you accountable and help you stay on track?

_____

Who do you know who is already doing what you want to be doing?

Celebrate It:

How will you acknowledge and reward yourself?

Reflections

Journal:

Doodles:

DAY 29

Personal Mission Statement

Notes from Yourself:

*Ask yourself, "What can I give?"
instead of "What can I get?"*

Love,
Yourself

Happy Warrior: Now that you know yourself and your Goals, and you know how to maintain the mindset to help you achieve them, boil it all down into an inspirational Personal Mission Statement.

Question: What is your Personal Mission Statement?

Personal Mission Statement

Example:

How do you want to be remembered?

As someone who inspires others.

How do you want people to describe you?

As a teacher or an expert.

Who/What matters most to you?

Helping people see their limitless potential.

How would you define "success" in your life?

Being of service to others.

Personal Mission Statement:

"To be inspiring coaches. And to be known for empowering our clients to elevate their consciousness and take their lives to the next level."
—John & Jami

Happy Warrior: Take some time with this, answer the questions below, and create an empowering Personal Mission Statement!

Question: What are you ready to own?

Personal Mission Statement

A Personal Mission Statement is a written declaration of your life's core purpose and focus. Read over the example page (left) and answer the questions below to create your own Personal Mission Statement.

How do you want to be remembered?

_____

_____

How do you want people to describe you?

_____

_____

Who/What matters most to you?

_____

_____

How would you define "success" in your life?

_____

_____

Personal Mission Statement

_____

_____

_____

_____

Reflections

Journal:

Doodles:

DAY 30

Journey Reflections

Notes from Yourself:

Every ending...is just another beginning.

Love,
Yourself

JOURNEY REFLECTIONS

How has *Happy Warrior* impacted your life?

_____
_____
_____
_____

What did you learn about your impact on others?

_____
_____
_____
_____

In what ways do you feel more empowered?

_____
_____
_____
_____

What tools will you use?

_____
_____
_____
_____

How will you maintain your progress?

_____
_____
_____
_____

Congratulations!
You've Arrived!

You have come a long way.

Well done! You've just acquired a set of tools and built a solid foundation to make lasting change and live your happiest life. The question is: "What now?" How do you incorporate everything you've learned into your normal life?

Hopefully you've incorporated some of this stuff, but it's impossible to implement all of it at once. Trust us, we've tried. Start by building small daily habits that you enjoy, you can keep up with, and give you a clear and immediate ROI. Over time you will find that life starts to flow more easily, you have more joy, more friends, and generally more love.

This is where the rubber meets the road. Putting these habits into practice will build sustainable change over the course of your life, but only if you do it! This is the path that you've already embarked on, the empowered path of a Happy Warrior.

With Gratitude,
John & Jami
Selfscription.com

Want More?

Happy Warrior, Your Practical Guide to a Happy Life, is powered by Selfscription®, designed to Free Your Mind and Take Your Life to the Next Level. Selfscription® has additional products and services to guide you on your happiness journey.

Products: Please visit Amazon.com/Selfscription

- Reflection Journal
- Pocket Planner
- Meeting Book
- Session Book

Services: to hire a coach, or to sign up to receive weekly Notes from Yourself, please visit Selfscription.com

With Gratitude,
John & Jami

Suggested Reading

The Four Agreements by Don Miguel Ruiz

The New Earth by Eckhart Tolle

The Power of Now by Eckhart Tolle

A Return to Love by Marianne Williamson

The Alchemist by Paulo Coelho

The Mastery of Love by Don Miguel Ruiz

The Gifts of Imperfection by Brené Brown

The Seven Habits of Highly Effective People by Stephen R. Covey

The 5 Love Languages by Gary Chapman

When Things Fall Apart by Pema Chodron

The Power of Habit by Charles Duhigg

Radical Forgiveness by Colin Tipping

What Color Is Your Parachute? by Richard N. Bolles

Autobiography of A Yogi by Paramahansa Yogananda

The Precious Present by Spencer Johnson M.D.

Mating in Captivity by Esther Perel

A Course in Miracles by The Foundation for Inner Peace

Quiet Leadership by David Rock

Catching the Big Fish by David Lynch

The Untethered Soul by Michael Singer

Daring Greatly by Brené Brown

Taming Your Gremlin by Rick Carson

Siddhartha by Herman Hesse

The War of Art by Steven Pressfield

Being Peace by Thich Nhat Hanh

Conversations with God by Neale Donald Walsch

Language of Letting Go by Melody Beattie

Broken Open by Elizabeth Lesser

Love Yourself Like Your Depends on It by Kamal Ravikant

Transformational Life Coaching by Cherie Carter-Scott

You Are a Badass by Jen Sincero

Energy Speaks by Lee Harris

The Missing Piece Meets the Big O by Shel Silverstein

Rebirth by Kamal Ravikant

A Curious Mind by Brian Grazer

10% Happier by Dan Harris

Lying by Sam Harris

The Artist's Way by Julia Cameron

About the Authors

John Kalinowski and Jami Bertini are NYU-certified coaches, authors, speakers, and mindset experts with nearly two decades of coaching experience between them. They joined forces in 2013 to write Selfscription®, a coaching program and workbook, which they have been using with their private clients for several years. In 2018, Selfscription® expanded to feature books, notebooks, workbooks, and inspirational quotes, all designed to Free Your Mind and Take Your Life to the Next Level. Selfscription® products will help you become the best you that you can be. Order yours today!

HAPPY WARRIOR

Made in the USA
Coppell, TX
21 May 2020

26152476R00129